THE ASSYRIANS

THE ASSYRIANS

ELAINE LANDAU

THE CRADLE OF CIVILIZATION
THE MILLBROOK PRESS
BROOKFIELD, CONNECTICUT

Cover photograph courtesy of Erich Lessing/
Art Resource, NY

Photographs courtesy of © Tor Eigeland: pp. 2-3; Erich
Lessing/Art Resource, NY: pp. 15, 25, 30, 45; © Robert
Frerck/Odyssey Productions/Chicago: p. 19; North
Wind Picture Archives: pp. 22, 32-33; Scala/Art
Resource, NY: p. 23; © British Museum: pp. 27, 44, 47
(both); The Granger Collection: p. 35; Giraudon/Art
Resource, NY: p. 38; Alinari/Art Resource, NY: p. 40;
© Silvio Fiore/SuperStock: p. 52.
Map by Joe LeMonnier.

Library of Congress Cataloging-in-Publication Data
Landau, Elaine.
The Assyrians / Elaine Landau.
p.   cm. – (The Cradle of civilization)
Includes bibliographical references and index.
Summary: Examines Assyria's growth from warlike city-state to
huge empire, through its conquest of all of Mesopotamia and
Egypt, and aspects of its culture.
ISBN 0-7613-0217-4 (lib. bdg.)
1. Assyria–Juvenile literature. [1. Assyria.] I. Title.
II. Series: Landau, Elaine. The cradle of civilization.
DS73.2.L29   1997
935–dc21   96-46899   CIP   AC

Published by The Millbrook Press, Inc.
2 Old New Milford Road,
Brookfield, Connecticut 06804

CONTENTS

THE ASSYRIANS

IN THE BEGINNING

Thousands of years ago there were no cities, countries, or governments as we know them today. Instead, small bands of people roamed the Earth living off the land. They were hunters and gatherers who were always on the move in search of wild game and fish as well as fruits and nuts to eat. These individuals didn't think of themselves as having a homeland. They were nomadic, or wandering, groups guided in their travels by the need to find food to survive.

No one knows precisely how or why things changed. What made some people trade the freedom to follow the animal herds for the strenuous task of tilling the soil? Although there are no definite answers, a number of theories have been suggested.

Historians note that at first just a few people may have separated from the wandering band. These were probably the weaker or smaller individuals who might have found it difficult to keep up with the rest. In addition, those who had been scorned or were unhappy with the group for some reason may have started to drop out as well.

It is also thought that women possibly played an important role in families settling down. Giving birth to and caring for young children while on the go must have been extremely difficult. Once women realized that remaining in one place would be best for both their offspring (children) and families, they may have been a powerful force behind this change of lifestyle.

There are numerous other unanswered questions as well. For example, when did the process of growing one's own food or planting and harvesting crops begin? Did a specific incident or change in the environment spur it on? Could some gathered seeds stored outdoors have accidentally taken root and become the first crop field? Or did the first "crops" spring up after some seeds left in a rubbish heap sprouted?

Naturally, this change didn't occur all at once. First, small groups of people settled down together, forming early villages that eventually grew into towns and cities. As these communities grew over the years, they changed. Societies complete with a written language, a code of law, and advanced technologies developed.

One of the places this first occurred was an area in what is now the Middle East known as Mesopotamia—a land between where the Tigris and Euphrates rivers empty into the Persian

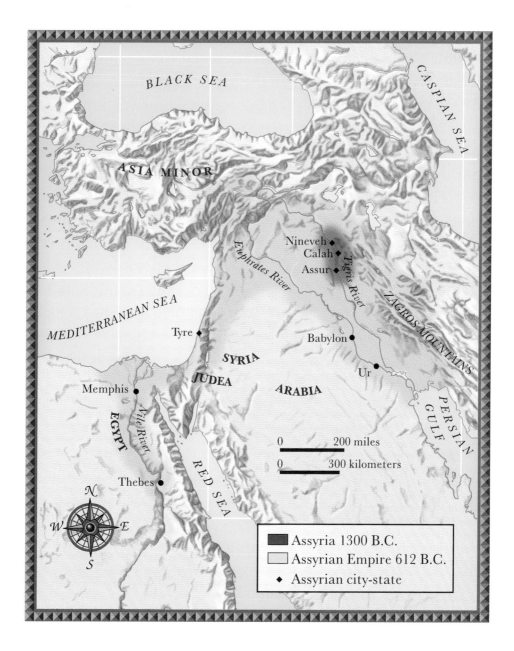

BLACK SEA

CASPIAN SEA

ASIA MINOR

Nineveh ◆
Calah ◆
Assur ◆

Euphrates River

Tigris River

ZAGROS MOUNTAINS

MEDITERRANEAN SEA

Tyre ◆

Babylon ●

SYRIA

JUDEA

Ur ●

ARABIA

PERSIAN GULF

Memphis ●

EGYPT

Nile River

| 0 | 200 miles |
| 0 | 300 kilometers |

Thebes ●

RED SEA

N
W E
S

| ■ Assyria 1300 B.C. |
| ☐ Assyrian Empire 612 B.C. |
| ◆ Assyrian city-state |

Gulf.[1] There on a hot, dry, windswept plain now referred to as a "cradle of civilization," some of the earliest cultures arose. Among these was Assyria, an area on the upper Tigris River in northern Mesopotamia. Another important region, known as Sumer, occupied 10,000 square miles (26,000 square kilometers) in southern Mesopotamia. Sumer later became Babylonia—a third accomplished Mesopotamian civilization.

The borders between these ancient areas were not always precisely drawn. Wars, political takeovers, and population shifts all served to intermingle the various peoples in the vicinity. Yet these three cultures remain distinct for their important contributions to the world. Ancient Mesopotamians invented the wheel, studied the stars and other heavenly bodies, and achieved important developments in mathematics, medicine, and architecture. They built cities, made advances in art and literature, and were the first people to develop a legal code.

For many years little was known about ancient Mesopotamia. Rain, floods, shifting sands, and other natural occurrences had completely erased its narrow, winding streets and its courtyards, religious towers, and magnificent palaces. But by the mid-nineteenth century, archaeologists had unearthed the clay tablets, pottery, tools, and building ruins of the Mesopotamians. To accomplish this, archaeological teams dug through huge mounds of soil, stripping away numerous layers of earth. Photographers took pictures of any articles found, while archaeologists interpreted when and how the various items were used. Specialists in ancient languages translated the writings on clay tablets, providing even more information on societies of the past. These clues enabled them to piece together a fascinating picture of the extremely advanced and industrious peoples who once inhabited this "cradle of civilization."

AN ANCIENT CIVILIZATION

t was an exciting day in the capital city of Assur. The king's soldiers were returning from a hard-fought military campaign beyond the country's borders. As expected, the army had been victorious. They had soundly defeated the enemy, and the newly conquered region would become part of the king's ever-growing empire.

The army returned with a wide array of wartime booty—goods that had been plundered from the losing nation. Gleaming gold and bronze vases, pitchers, and cups were presented, as well as beautifully carved ivory furniture, decorated daggers, rings made of precious metals, and long ivory elephant tusks.[2] When a distant land was overtaken, unusual animals such as two-humped camels, elephants, or crocodiles might be included in the returning soldiers' parade to the royal palace.

This stone carving from an Assyrian palace
shows victorious soldiers returning from war
carrying the heads of their enemies.

Such scenes were not uncommon. The king's soldiers were exceedingly well trained and practiced in the art of warfare. Even as young boys, they had learned the importance of battlefield victory. This was Assyria—an ancient land known for its fierce fighters and empire builders.

Assyria, which existed from the fourteenth century B.C. to 612 B.C., was situated on the upper Tigris River. To its north lay the Armenian Mountains, while the Zagros Mountains and the hills of Iran bordered Assyria to the east.

Although its summers were usually hot and dry, Assyria still had more rainfall and a considerably cooler climate than neighboring areas to its south and west. Yet through the centuries, numerous Assyrian rulers waged elaborate military campaigns to overtake these regions, as well as to seize highly desirable trade routes further west to the Mediterranean Sea. These land and sea conquests meant a great deal to the Assyrians. At the height of their power, the empire had acquired a vast assortment of valuable resources, including timber, grain, and precious stones and metals. It also made Assyria a well-known and feared power to be dealt with.

3

LIFE IN ASSYRIA

The Assyrian king was the supreme ruler of the land. It was a role that his heir to the throne, the crown prince, began preparing for from an early age. Once the crown prince was old enough to leave his mother, the young man went to live in a palace known as the House of Succession. There he had a court much like his father's, complete with advisers who schooled him in what he would need to know as king. By the time he took the throne, it was hoped that the Assyrian crown prince would be a skilled horseman, hunter, fighter, and ruler.

Being close to an Assyrian king could greatly enhance a person's lot in life. And sometimes there seemed to be no limit to what someone might do to stay in the king's good graces. However, getting close to the king was never easy. At the palace he was usually surrounded either by official advisers or his harem (group of wives). Anyone wishing to see the king first had to go through the majordomo–the head official responsible for arranging audiences (meetings) with the Assyrian ruler. And as palace officials usually only received modest wages, bribes to do so were regularly offered and accepted.

No one doubted that such measures were worthwhile. Often the king granted large parcels of farmland to influential Assyrian men in good standing with the royal court. When these men died, the land supposedly was returned to the king. But if the family was highly regarded by the king and sufficiently impressive gifts had been presented to him, the estate was redeeded to the heir of the deceased.

Common people farmed the land for the powerful individuals who held title to it. These farmers lived in small villages on the estates where they grew barley, sesame, corn, wheat, and other crops. They also raised sheep, goats, and cattle, and produced dairy products.

While the waters of the Tigris River and its streams helped to keep the land fertile, farmers still had to irrigate (direct water to the fields). Sometimes they dug canals to channel the water where it was needed. In cases where elevated fields required

The Tigris River Valley was a fertile area. Farmers used the river's waters to irrigate the surrounding farmland, even land that was elevated.

irrigation, the Assyrians used specially designed machines to raise the water. During the early spring it was important to remain alert to possible flooding. As the weather grew warmer, heavy rains, along with melting snows from surrounding mountains, often caused Assyria's waters to overflow.

While Assyria had farmland, large city centers such as Assur, Nineveh, and Calah arose at various times in its history. City life in Assyria differed greatly from farm life. Artisans, tradespeople, and craftsworkers usually worked out of these centers, while the king also had a palace in Assyria's capital city.

Whether living on a farm or in a city, dwellings for common people in ancient Assyria weren't very fancy. Usually these were quickly constructed small brick huts with roofs made of tree branches gathered from the riverbanks. The Assyrians made their own bricks from the earth. They moistened clumps of thick, rich soil, adding some chopped straw to hold them together. After being shaped into squares and dried in the sun, the bricks were ready for use.

Royal Assyrian palaces, sacred temples, and public buildings, on the other hand, were more elaborate. These sturdy structures were erected on 40-foot (12-meter) -high brick platforms and had roofs made of wooden beams held together by a mud plaster spread on the outside. The buildings' walls were made of thick layers of sun-dried bricks covered by large alabaster slabs. Using bright colors, talented artists painted the slabs with scenes from Assyria's past. The walls of these special buildings served as history books of sorts, often revealing the daring exploits and conquests that the Assyrians were proud of.

The main entrances to Assyrian palaces and temples were decorated with huge sculptures of winged lions or bulls with human heads. Large statues of Assyrian gods or high priests also were placed over some of the entrances to the chambers within.

Besides enhancing their buildings, the artisans and craftspeople of Assyrian cities were vital in furthering the magnificence of the king and his court. While common Assyrians dressed plainly in sandals and long tunics (loose-fitting garments gathered at the waist), the king, court officials, and other people of importance dressed elegantly. The king wore a beautifully embroidered gown trimmed with fringe. It was tied at the waist with a long decorative cord that had tassels at the ends. Over the gown he wore a splendid robelike garment that was usually left open at the front.

Assyrian kings and officials also had numerous pieces of jewelry. The king often wore one or more necklaces along with several bracelets on his arms and wrists. Some of the jewelry had brilliant stones and clasps shaped like lion heads, and clearly reflected the superior craftsmanship of the Assyrian artists.

Artists and craftspersons also created various headpieces to be worn on special occasions. Assyrians usually wore their hair long, woven into a number of small braids pushed back behind the ears. Some of the hair was left unbraided and

The clothing of Assyrian people reflected their standing in society. Common people dressed much more plainly than kings or other official persons.

This ivory sculpture of a woman's head shows the fine detail and skill that Assyrian craftsmen brought to their work.

lying on the shoulders in ringlet curls. To keep their hair in place, Assyrians wore headbands. Common people usually had leather headbands, but many well-off Assyrians wore ornate headbands set with precious stones. However, only the king wore a tall pointed headpiece that was exquisitely decorated.

Besides making beautiful garments, jewelry, and head ornaments, Assyrian artisans also produced a variety of leather goods, including shields, horse harnesses, chair and chariot covers, and skins for holding liquids. There were also potters who created fine bowls, jugs, and pitchers, as well as sculptors who worked with stone, wood, and ivory. Some of the ancient ivory work was especially bold and exquisite. Sculptors carved magnificent female heads from ivory and used thin layers of gold on the sculptured hair and paint to accent the eyes and eyebrows. It also was not uncommon for the throne of an Assyrian king to be decorated with small carved ivory pieces.

Assyrian cities were protected from enemy attacks by high, thick brick walls. Above the few entrance gates in the walls were raised guard towers from which armed soldiers kept watch. Fighting skills were extremely important to the Assyrians. Whether they lived in the city or countryside, young Assyrian boys were taught to ride a horse shortly after they began to walk. Before long, they would learn to shoot a bow and arrow.

Assyrian kings prided themselves on being exceptionally brave and able hunters. Often they went off to the plains to hunt dangerous animals. Elephants, wild bulls, and lions made especially exciting targets because of their size and ferocity when challenged. The king also publicly displayed his courage, physical coordination, and hunting prowess in staged royal lion hunts. For these much-anticipated events, the Assyrians maintained spacious animal preserves known as parks or paradises. Such enclosed areas were well stocked with lions, tigers, wild boars, antelopes, and other animals. During a hunt, a lion or other large animal was released for the king to either shoot down with a bow and arrow or kill with a large dagger.[3] Although most Assyrian kings were good hunters and fight-

Hunting wild animals was a favorite sport of Assyrian kings. Here, King Assurnasirpal hunts a lion from his chariot. Although the kings were skilled hunters, they were backed up by expert spearmen, as shown here.

ers, their safety during a hunt was always assured by a line of expert bow- and spearmen standing nearby. At times, the king invited other influential men to take part in the hunt with him. This was considered a great honor reserved for a chosen few.

A great deal of effort went into keeping the parks filled with an array of animals. Some lions were captured high in the mountains and shipped to the parks for the hunts. Others were born in captivity and raised solely for this purpose.

To the Assyrians, the killing of a lion was symbolic of defeating their enemies in battle. The king's wisdom, fitness, and courage were respected and admired by his people. Numerous hunting scenes were depicted in Assyrian sculpture, wall murals, and the embroidery on their finest garments.

But while hunting and fighting skills were of prime importance to the Assyrians, young males were expected to master other tasks as well. To prepare for later life, children learned farming techniques from their parents or worked in craft or trade shops. Before the age of ten, Assyrian boys from wealthy families might be tutored by a local scribe or priest. Such children were taught the basics of cuneiform script—a form of writing consisting of wedge-shaped symbols on clay tablets used by the Assyrians and other ancient peoples to record matters of law, medicine, history, and other subjects. Assyrian kings sometimes ordered that these clay tablets be preserved in large libraries constructed especially for that purpose.

Although war and conquest were the Assyrians' first priorities, scribes held an important position in society.

Well-bred Assyrian boys usually did not study cuneiform script to become expert scribes. However, someone who hoped to eventually have an important position at the king's court had to be able to write letters, keep accurate financial accounts, and record events.[4] But knowledge meant little in Assyria if a young man wasn't a fearless fighter. A promising teenager serving at the palace might be given the honor of running alongside the king's chariot in battle. Later on he might serve on horseback in the cavalry. In any case, he believed that the best thing he could do for his king and homeland was to help enhance Assyria's glory by fighting.

Often the Assyrian appetite for challenges and battle was evident in how their leaders ruled the country and expanded the empire. Among the outstanding kings in Assyria's history is Tiglath Pileser I, who, after coming to power in 1115 B.C., ushered Assyria into an era of greatness. Tiglath Pileser I was often characterized as brutal, and was usually successful in battle. Among his numerous contributions to Assyria itself was the restoration of the main temple at the capital city of Assur and the establishment of numerous parks.

King Assurnasirpal II, who reigned in the ninth century B.C., was another notable Assyrian ruler. He added a sizable number of provinces to Assyria's empire and captured highly valued trade routes to the Mediterranean Sea.

Following the reign of Tiglath Pileser I, Assyria had declined somewhat for about two centuries, but Assurnasirpal II helped it to reach new levels of conquest. He also established a new capital city, Calah, where he built a magnificent royal palace. He described the structure as "a palace of cedar, cypress, juniper, boxwood, mulberry, pistachio-wood, and tamarisk, for my royal dwelling and for my lordly pleasure for all time I founded therein. Beasts of the mountains and of the seas of white limestone and alabaster I fashioned and set them up in its gates. I made it suitable, I made it glorious....And silver, gold, tin, bronze, and iron, the spoil from my hand from the lands which I had brought under my sway, in great quantities I took and placed them therein."[5]

Assurnasirpal II gave superb banquets at the palace to which people were invited from throughout Assyria's vast realm. At times these feasts lasted as long as ten days. On one such occasion the king's many guests consumed more than 2,000 oxen and 16,000 sheep, as well as numerous roasted game birds and countless kegs of wine. During his reign, Assurnasirpal II put through an advanced irrigation system to bring additional water to the distant rural areas of Assyria.

Assurnasirpal II's son, King Shalmaneser III, came to power in 858 B.C. and ruled for thirty-five years. He spent much of his time on the battlefield, but he wasn't always successful. He also had to deal with rebellion within his own court and overall feelings of unrest in the countryside. Shalmaneser III's descent from the throne marked the start of an Assyrian decline that lasted for

King Tiglath Pileser III was one of the most successful Assyrian kings. He devised a plan to keep track of Assyria's large empire, and thus to keep control of it for a time.

about seventy-five years. During that period, Assyria lost control over much of the territory it had acquired.

The situation improved by the middle of the eighth century B.C., when King Tiglath Pileser III came to power. Tiglath Pileser III recaptured the lost territory and added new lands. He established a system of messenger relays that allowed him to keep abreast of matters even in distant parts of the realm. Tiglath Pileser III also greatly enhanced the army, reorganizing the divisions and swelling the ranks with soldiers from captured city-states and mercenary forces (soldiers for hire).

The power and splendor that Tiglath Pileser III restored to Assyria lasted for nearly the next one hundred years. Yet that period was not completely free of problems. But by the time King Sargon II of Assyria came to power in 721 B.C., Assyria's hold on its territory had seriously weakened and much of the empire was in a near state of revolt. Though he attempted further conquests, there were often more pressing issues to attend to.

Before the end of his reign, Sargon II moved Assyria's capital from Calah to a site known as Nineveh. There he built a great city and a royal palace that supposedly even surpassed the beauty of the royal residence that Assurnasirpal II had designed. But shortly after the completion of his breathtaking palace, King Sargon II was killed in battle.

Although Sargon II's son, Sennacherib, made Nineveh one of the most splendid cities of the ancient world, this ruler may be best remembered for destroying Babylon—a great center of culture and art to Assyria's south. Eight years after Babylon's demise, Sennacherib was murdered by one of his own sons.

Another of Sennacherib's sons, Esarhaddon, took the throne following his father's death. Although Esarhaddon only ruled

Under the reign of King Sargon II, Nineveh became Assyria's capital. This view of the city shows the splendid royal palace.

for eleven years, he accomplished a great deal. He rebuilt Babylon, quelled rebellious elements in the territories, and in 671 B.C. extended Assyria's reach to another continent by invading Egypt.

LAW AND RELIGION

The king was the undisputed leader of Assyria. Serving as chief priest as well as head of the empire, he was believed to be both royalty and God's chosen earthly representative. The lives of many Assyrians either directly or indirectly revolved around the king's wishes.

But were Assyrian kings really as free as they seemed? Although they held the title of chief priest, these kings weren't active religious leaders. In keeping with Assyrian religious rites and dictates, they were allowed to enter the sacred temples only under very specific conditions.

An Assyrian king's life was greatly influenced by high priests who were supposedly able to read omens (signs of the future) and royal astrologers (individuals who claim to be able to foretell events through the placement of the moon and stars). Royal rulers carefully heeded their advice, believing that only these powerful religious men could see

A priest, dressed in the head and wings of an eagle, anoints King Assurnasirpal II in this stone carving. Although the king was the undisputed ruler, his actions were greatly influenced by high priests.

Assyria's destiny and that of the throne. After forecasting an ill-fated event, it was up to the high priests and astrologers to determine the best course of action. This could cause the king a considerable degree of inconvenience and discontent. They might suggest that he fast (eat nothing) for several days, remain by himself in a room for some time, or even cut off all his hair and shave his beard.

Magic, rituals, and fortune-telling were an important part of Assyrian religion. These ancient people believed that thousands of deities (gods) capable of influencing a person's fate existed. Such powerful beings could also wreak havoc with the empire through storms, droughts, fires, and other natural disasters. However, most common people were only concerned with a few gods whom they thought directly affected everyday life. Assur, for whom one of Assyria's capital cities was named, was regarded as the most important god. Lesser, but still prominent deities included Ninurta, the god of war and the hunt, and Ishtar, the goddess of love.

The Assyrians believed that harmful spirits existed all around them. These evil spirits could lurk anywhere but were especially drawn to deserts, graveyards, and palace ruins. Pregnant women or those who had just given birth were thought to be especially vulnerable to these nasty spirits. When infants died suddenly it was generally attributed to these spirits—but most other serious illnesses that befell the Assyrians were thought to be caused by demons as well.

The cruel creatures were said to be extremely swift-footed as well as able to ride on the wind or float on a water drop. Yet demons were believed to also have shortcomings. Supposedly, they weren't very smart and could be easily deceived.

For protection from these dangers, the Assyrians appealed to benevolent, or kindhearted, spirits to protect them. The good spirits were represented by the human-headed lion and bull statues posted over many of the entranceways of their building and city walls.

Assyrians who were able to pay the fee sought help from priests specially trained in magic. Many believed that these priests could trap a demon in a pottery jar or use magic to force a demon to torment an animal instead of the human it had focused on. Assyrians also looked to such priests to fend off evil spells cast by witches and warlocks.

Assyrian temples, located in the cities, were large magnificent buildings run by a sizable staff of both men and women. Each important god had its own temple. Priests and priestesses performed sacred rituals and sacrifices under the direction of a high priest. Many religious festival days were celebrated as well.

Others who worked at the temple were not in the priesthood. Singers and musicians provided music, while various staff members maintained the grounds and secured the necessary materials for religious rites. There were sword bearers to sacrifice animals, and artisans to create statues used in special religious ceremonies.

This statue of a bull with a human head stood guard at the gate of the palace of King Sargon II. The figure represents a benevolent spirit meant to protect the king.

Assyrian religion centered more on mystical questions and beliefs than on everyday practical matters. Therefore, between 1450 and 1250 B.C., the Assyrians devised a legal code known as the Middle Assyrian Laws for guidance in such matters. The clay tablets dealing with these regulations that have been recovered largely reveal the behavior required of women.

The code shows that a woman was not considered a man's equal and was forced to be subservient to her husband, father, and brothers. For example, neither married women nor widows were permitted to go out in public unless their faces were covered with a veil. Another law stated that if a woman took an object from her husband's house and gave it to another person (either male or female), the husband had the right to punish both his wife and the individual receiving the item. A man was also permitted to flog (beat) his wife or "injure [cut or otherwise mutilate] her ears" for minor wrongdoing.[6]

Assyrian law dealt with disputes between neighbors over land and farm animals as well. If such disagreements couldn't be settled by the persons involved, they went before an officer of the administration to decide the matter. This was necessary because ancient Assyria did not have courts or judges as we know them. The officer of the administration listened to witnesses from both sides and examined any related evidence. If the officer was unable to arrive at a verdict, an accused person might have to be judged by the river god. Someone facing judgment by the river god was required to jump into the river. If the

This carving of an Assyrian cavalry unit shows the elaborate weapons, chariots, and dress that the warriors used in battle.

individual drowned, it was assumed that he had lied under oath and was guilty. But if he survived, his innocence was thought to be proven, and his accuser was put to death.

Assyrian law allowed for severe punishments other than death. Someone guilty of a serious crime might be blinded or thrown into prison for an extended time. Yet the Assyrian legal system wasn't actually as brutal as it might seem. Instead of having a hand cut off or being jailed for a prolonged period, a guilty person could pay the injured party a sum of money and escape the punishment entirely.

There were other options for those who did not have the funds to buy their way out of such difficult situations. A person could avoid a long prison term by agreeing to serve as his victim's slave for a shorter time. This solution was often preferred by the wronged party since the free labor somewhat compensated for the injury or financial loss suffered.

THE WARRING
ASSYRIANS

At the height of its empire, Assyria was well known for its tireless warriors. The state had begun to develop militarily centuries before, when it was forced to defend itself from attacks from warlike neighbors. Finding that superior battle skills could afford it both security and riches from surrounding areas, Assyria continued to build up its forces as well as take an aggressive role in the frays.

At first there wasn't a formal Assyrian army. But every young able-bodied man was expected to fight when called upon to do so. However, wealthy and influential men were usually allowed to either have a slave serve in their place or make a substantial payment to the king in lieu of serving.

In time the Assyrians organized a large, impressive fighting force. By the ninth century B.C., they were launching yearly spring military campaigns to expand their growing empire. The Assyrians prided themselves on keeping a fully-trained standing army ready for action at any time. This was necessary to crush budding revolts in previously conquered areas. As commander and chief of the military, the Assyrian king scattered military units throughout the acquired territory. Near the empire's outer borders, substantial forts were constructed to underscore the conqueror's presence. If a widespread emergency arose, Assyrian soldiers were reinforced by troops from some of the provinces within the empire. Although precise figures are unavailable, it's estimated that at one point hundreds of thousands of men were at the Assyrian king's disposal.

Marching forth in an organized, well-disciplined manner, an Assyrian troop movement could be a fearsome spectacle. First came a group of soldiers bearing banners, followed by the king's priests and astrologers, who were there to advise the king on forthcoming events. Next came the Assyrian king, riding in his richly ornamented chariot. Since these vehicles did not have seats, the king stood upright during the attack, regally facing his enemy. The chariots were pulled by two or three well-groomed horses decked out in splendid finery. Each horse had a large plume attached to its headdress as well as tassels draped on its forehead and around its neck. The animals' harnesses were studded with precious stones, and their bits (mouthpieces) were made of solid gold.

The king was surrounded by a large group of well-armed horsemen and foot soldiers. Besides engaging in combat, it was their responsibility to protect the king. Behind them was a mas-

Above: A dramatic battle scene shows the bombardment of a walled city using a sophisticated device that resembles a modern-day tank. Facing page: Assyrian warriors scale the walls of an Egyptian city during King Assurnasirpal's siege. Egypt was added to the Assyrian empire, where it remained for a time.

sive band of soldiers, including high-ranking officers in chariots, the cavalry, infantry (foot soldiers), and small specialized units of spies, expert bowmen, and scouts who were familiar with the territory.

Assyrian soldiers going to war were always well armed. Depending on their role in the assault, these fighters carried an

assortment of weapons, including slings of rope and leather with which to hurl stones and rocks, as well as swords, daggers, and bows and arrows. Assyrian archers used two types of bows—a short, slightly curved one and an angled one. The arrows, made of reeds with metal barbs, were carried in a sack slung over the shoulder. While on the march, an archer placed the larger bow over his head and carried it on his shoulders. The king's bows and arrows were always carried by an attendant who remained close by.

The Assyrians used various types of shields to protect themselves. Medium-sized circular shields made of either animal skins or metals such as gold or silver were popular in Assyria's early days. But later on they traded their smaller shields for larger ones that covered the entire body. During a siege, a bowman on foot couldn't carry his own shield since he needed both hands to aim and shoot. Therefore, a shield bearer remained at his side, covering the archer with a large shield while carrying a dagger to protect himself. Archers on horseback rode with a second horseman to hold and guide the archer's horse during an advance.

Assyrian soldiers dressed for battle according to their rank and duties. The higher-ranking officers who rode chariots into battle wore long coats of armor reaching to their knees or ankles. Their heads were protected by round metal caps or helmets. As time passed, these helmets became increasingly elaborate, with curved crests or plumes on top. Assyrian army officers were

Although the Assyrians were often described as bloodthirsty in battle and ruthless captors, these scenes of war prisoners (left), and the deportation of women and children (below), seem to suggest otherwise.

especially well outfitted for battle, and the young soldiers shielding the king were decked out in full armor as well. It was crucial that the royal shield bearers—who were the king's first defense against enemy arrows—not be easily slain.

During major strikes, Assyrian kings prided themselves on leading their forces into battle. However, preparing for the trip involved a great deal of work on the part of their court and family. Regardless of the distance, the king was accompanied by one or more wives, children, royal advisers, palace officials, nobles, musicians, and a large number of servants.[7]

Advancing Assyrian troops were further burdened with the necessary materials and instruments of war. Battering rams to break down city gates and walls were essential if the Assyrians were to succeed. They also brought along large devices made of wood and animal hide to catapult oversized rocks past enemy defenses. The soldiers also had long poles with thick iron ends to knock stones out of the enemy's walls; axes were useful for this task as well.

Moving an army and all its gear to distant regions wasn't easy. Assyrian engineers tried to find ways to transport the larger weapons without slowing down the troops. They also had to build temporary bridges when they came to rivers or broad streams. In addition, roads often needed to be constructed through barely passable mountain ranges.

Providing food for the huge Assyrian army was another daunting task. Supplies such as oil and corn were usually taken along. If the troops were headed for a dry, infertile region where grazing space was scarce, hay and extra corn for the horses were brought. The Assyrians valued their horses highly and used them for riding and farmwork in addition to warfare. During wartime campaigns, horses were essential to both the cavalry and chariot drivers.

Whenever possible, the Assyrian army lived off the land while traveling. They picked fruits from local orchards and hunted wild animals for meat. When passing through a region that was already part of the empire, the province's local officials were expected to feed the troops and horses. And when enemy territory was taken, soldiers could raid the grain stores and food stocks of those who were defeated.

Once the Assyrian army neared its final destination, it set up camp. The battering rams, catapults, and various other weapons were drawn up to the enemy's outer gates. Assyrian troops might try several approaches to get past the city walls. Flaming torches would be hurled at the structure, while soldiers used axes to rip apart the bricks. But the most common way to gain entrance was for the soldiers to scale the walls with ladders. These soldiers were protected by expert bowmen on the ground shooting at enemy archers defending their territory.

There are contradictory accounts of how the Assyrians treated the peoples they conquered. At times the Assyrians have been described as ruthless, bloodthirsty empire builders. Assyrian King Tiglath Pileser I's account of how he vanquished a region was thought typical of the Assyrian fighting style: "With their twenty-thousand warriors and their five Kings I fought…and I defeated them.… Their blood I let flow in the valleys and on the high levels of the mountains. I cut off their heads and outside their cities, like heaps of grain, I piled them.… I burned their cities with fire, I demolished them, I cleared them away…."[8]

Some ancient murals show Assyrians burning conquered cities and slaughtering their populations. They are shown beheading victims or plunging daggers into their hearts. Assyrian soldiers also were said to sometimes torture defeated peoples before enslaving them.

However, there are historians who dispute this view of the Assyrians. While admitting that the Assyrians were fearless conquerors, these scholars argue that the Assyrians were not overly harsh in their wartime policies and practices. They stress that when Assyria launched a fierce campaign against a particular city, it was done to intimidate the rulers of nearby states they hoped to conquer soon afterward. Wishing to avoid a crushing defeat at the hands of the Assyrian army, surrounding areas often surrendered without a struggle. Avoiding costly wartime campaigns saved the Assyrians valuable manpower, time and money.

After taking over a new region, the local ruler was usually left in charge. But now his actions would be controlled by Assyria's king. To ensure that things went smoothly, an Assyrian representative was stationed at the conquered people's palace.

Often, treaties between the defeated country and Assyria were drawn up to clearly define the responsibilities of the conquered people. These agreements might state the role of the Assyrian representative in pertinent matters, including conferences he would attend and activities he was to oversee. As one such agreement designed by an Assyrian king stated, "You shall not open up a letter that I send you without the Qipu-official [the Assyrian representative]. If the Qipu-official is not at hand, you shall await him [and then] open [it]."[9]

When a conquered province tried to revolt, the Assyrians usually reacted immediately. If the rebellious group proved difficult to crush, the Assyrians sometimes resorted to a type of deportation in which the troublesome group was relocated to a distant part of the empire. While they remained far from their home base of support, their landholdings were taken over by newcomers from still other areas of the empire. Assyrian administrators, along with an increased military presence, were at the rebellion site for a time to make certain that things remained quiet. It seemed as if the Assyrians had mastered the art of military conquest down to the last detail.

Well-preserved ruins of the walls of Nineveh are all that remain of this once-splendid capital city of Assyria.

THE FALL

Eventually the Assyrian empire reached remarkable heights. The army conquered nearly all of western Asia and, after quelling discontent in Syria and Judea, marched into Egypt. From there it traveled farther south to invade what today are the African nations of Libya and Ethiopia. With such outstanding successes, it seemed as if Assyria would never fail.

Yet a number of factors were actually working against Assyria. At one point, its empire spanned a distance of more than 1,000 miles (1,600 kilometers)—an immense area for any ancient state to control for an extended period. With its acquired territory so widespread, it became exceedingly difficult for Assyrian rulers to stamp out the rebellions that sprang up on various fronts at the same time. As a result, Assyria's strong grasp on its empire began to weaken. Its position as a major power was further hampered by the numerous wealthy landholders who had become more concerned with their estates and revenues than with Assyria's welfare.

Then near the end of the seventh century B.C. the region's balance of power began to shift. Determined to seize the opportunity, the Medes, a little-known people of the Iranian plateau, joined forces with the Chaldeans of Babylonia to topple an already weakened Assyria. They destroyed the magnificent Assyrian cities of Nineveh and Assur, as well as other important Assyrian centers. Unlike it had done in the past, Assyria never recovered.

In the centuries that followed, the area that had been Assyria was invaded by a number of foreign powers, including the Greeks, Arabs, and Turks. When Britain defeated Turkey in World War I, the land fell into British hands. They renamed the region Iraq and established an Arab government that operated under British control. However, many Iraqis bitterly resented the British role in their lives. And in response to an ongoing Iraqi freedom movement, Britain finally granted Iraq its independence in 1932.

A visitor to modern-day Iraq would never know that Assyria once existed in the country's north. All that is left of this once great military power are the recovered ruins that reveal its dramatic story.

IMPORTANT DATES

1500-200 B.C.   Early Assyrian history is marked by periods of domination by foreign powers followed by Assyria regaining its independence.

1115 B.C.   Tiglath Pileser I leads Assyria into an era of greatness. Besides being a powerful conqueror, he restores many of Assyria's palaces and the main temple.

1077 B.C.   Assyria enters a period of decline. Much of its territory is lost to invading tribes.

884 B.C.   Assurnasirpal II restores Assyria's empire and adds valuable trade routes to the Mediterranean Sea.

858 B.C.   Shalmaneser III rules during a time of unrest and rebellion in Assyria. Following his descent from the throne, Assyria begins to decline.

745 B.C.	Tiglath Pileser III returns a power and splendor to Assyria that lasts for nearly the next one hundred years.
689 B.C.	Assyrian ruler Sennacherib destroys Babylon.
612 B.C.	Iranian Medes join forces with the Chaldeans of Babylonia to topple Assyria. Assyria never recovers.

NOTES

1. Arthur Cotterell, ed., *The Encyclopedia of Civilizations* (New York: Mayflower Books, Inc., 1980), p. 72.

2. Andre Parrot, *The Arts of Assyria* (New York: Golden Press, 1961), p. 105.

3. Cotterell, p. 106.

4. Jorgen Laessoe, *People of Ancient Assyria* (New York: Barnes & Noble Inc., 1963), p. 32.

5. Samuel Noah Kramer and the Editors of Time-Life Books, *Cradle of Civilization* (Alexandria, VA: Time-Life Books, 1978), p. 58.

6. H. W. F. Saggs, *Everyday Life in Babylonia & Assyria* (New York: G. P. Putnam's Sons, 1967), p. 152.

7. Shirley Glubok, ed., *Digging in Assyria* (New York: Macmillan, 1970), p. 115.

8. Kramer, p. 57.

9. Saggs, p. 118.

GLOSSARY

artisan–a trained or skilled worker or craftsperson

astrologer–an individual who claims to understand the connection between heavenly bodies and someone's destiny

battering ram–a long wide beam used in ancient warfare to break down gates and walls

bit–the metal mouthpiece of a horse's bridle

booty–a prize or reward resulting from a war victory

chariot–a two-wheeled vehicle used in ancient times for war or racing

cuneiform script–a form of writing used by the Assyrians and other ancient people consisting of wedge-shaped symbols cut into clay tablets

deities–gods

havoc–disorder, confusion, or destruction

omen–a sign of the future

park (also known as a *paradise*)–an enclosed area containing a spacious animal preserve that the Assyrians kept well stocked with lions, tigers, wild boars, and antelopes, used for the king's royal hunts

province–a region located some distance from the capital or major cities

ritual–a ceremony performed in a prescribed manner over a period of time

tunic–a loose-fitting garment gathered at the waist

warlock–a sorcerer, or male witch

FURTHER READING

Avi-Yonah, Michael. *Dig This! How Archaeologists Uncover Our Past.* Minneapolis: Runestone, 1993.

Coblence, Jean-Michel. *The Earliest Cities.* Morristown, NJ: Silver Burdett, 1987.

Corbishley, Mike. *Secret Cities.* New York: Lodestar Books, 1989.

Cox, Phil Roxbee. *Who Were the First People?* Tulsa, OK: EDC Publications, 1995.

Gallant, Roy A. *Lost Cities.* Danbury, CT: Franklin Watts, Inc., 1985.

Hackwell, W. John. *Digging to the Past: Excavations in Ancient Lands.* New York: Scribner's, 1986.

Krupp, Robin Rector. *Let's Go Traveling.* New York: Morrow Junior Books, 1992.

Martell, Hazel. *The Kingfisher Book of the Ancient World: From the Ice Age to the Fall of Rome.* New York: Kingfisher, 1995.

Maynard, Christopher. *Incredible Buried Treasure*. New York: Covent Garden Books, 1994.

Merriman, Nick. *Early Humans*. New York: Knopf, 1989.

Millard, Anne. *How People Lived*. New York: Dorling Kindersley, 1993.

Oliphant, Margaret. *The Earliest Civilizations*. New York: Facts on File, 1993.

Trease, Geoffrey. *Hidden Treasure*. New York: Lodestar Books, 1989.

Wilkinson, Philip. *The Master Builders*. New York: Chelsea House, 1994.

INDEX